I0072386

About the author:

Kurt Felgemacher worked as a Civil Engineer for over 30 years, 27 of which were with the New York State Department of Transportation (NYSDOT). He obtained his B.S. in Civil Engineering in 1986, and a Masters in Business Administration (MBA) in 1988, both from the State University of New York at Buffalo. He holds a Professional Engineering license in New York State since 1992 and has experience serving as an expert witness in transportation litigation.

Starting out, he invested in his company's Employee Stock Ownership Program (ESOP) at his first professional job, and then later in the Deferred Compensation Program at the NYSDOT. Having been an avid reader of the Wall Street Journal throughout his working years, he gradually added wealth by self-guided investments through banks, brokerage accounts, and real-estate.

He is happily married, has three adult children and resides in

Amherst, New York.

This book is for informational purposes only, it is not

intended to make your specific personal financial decisions.

Investing and financial decisions have inherent risk, and in no

way is the author responsible for any financial losses by

individuals.

Copyright 2025 by Kurt Felgemacher

All rights reserved. No part of this publication may be reproduced, distributed, or transmitted in any form or by any means, including photocopying, recording, or other electronic or mechanical methods, without the prior permission of the author, except as permitted by U.S. copyright law. Chapters 12 and 13 can be copied per U.S. copyright law as they are public domain information. For permission requests please email the author, Kurt Felgemacher at kfelgs@netzero.net

Published by

ISBN

First Edition, 2025

Concise Guide to Wealth, Social Security, and Medicare: What Everyone Always Likes To Have - W.E.A.L.T.H.

Kurt Felgemacher – First Edition

Acknowledgement

Thanks to my sister Karen Braun who supported me in writing this book.

Chapter 12 – Social Security and Chapter 13 – Medicare of this book are public domain information taken from their respective federal government websites.

This guidebook is dedicated to all hard-working men and women striving for financial success.

Table of Contents

Introduction

This book is not about get rich quick schemes, rather, prudent proven methods that lead individuals to financial success over the long haul. Wealth building usually involves compounding interest on investments, the appreciation of assets and money saving techniques that accumulate over a long period of time, slow and steady. The Concise Guide to Wealth offers many insights that will hasten the creation of wealth through savvy business and financial techniques.

Think of wealth building as a blueprint for the future which maximizes your ability to accumulate wealth. We must be diligent and smart regarding our financial investments by creating a portfolio that will provide the tools that will bring

us future prosperity.

The Concise Guide to Wealth will teach you the basic tools of

wealth building, which over time, will bring you great

financial success and a happy retirement.

Chapter 1

Formal Education

The value of a formal education and/or training with special skills (i.e. computer technology, building trades, automotive tech, etc.) is undeniably one of the most powerful money-making tools that can be afforded to an individual. Schools not only teach us useful information for increasing our ability to think logically, they also teach us how to learn.

Elementary, Junior and Senior High Schools, training centers, and Universities increase the ability of the mind to comprehend and execute critical thinking. It is important to increase one's own ability to gain knowledge of almost any kind with the realization that learning and the acquisition of new and updated skill sets, should continue throughout your working life.

Examples:

- High Schools, College Degrees and Diplomas

- Training certificates

- State or Federal Licensure

Any formalized training that can help to obtain a lucrative vocation is "money in the bank".

In summary, the knowledge and skills gained through education increases your odds of obtaining wealth.

Suggestion: When deciding on an education, consider the factors likely to give you the best return-on-investment (ROI). These can include such things as tuition cost, pay scale for your degree (occupation), scholarships available, quality of education, job opportunities, and tuition help from family.

Chapter 2

Taxes

Understanding tax implications for the various types of

financial transactions enhances maximizing wealth. Keeping

profits sheltered from both state, federal and local taxes

accelerates the accumulation of personal assets. Maximizing

financial prosperity involves gaining an understanding of tax

laws, including but not limited to: tax brackets, tax

deductions and credits, tax free and tax limiting investments, and retirement tax strategies. Finding out the best ways to avoid or reduce taxes on your earnings is an effective strategy to for building wealth.

Examples:

- Traditional and Roth IRA's – delay paying taxes on your earnings (earned income) or avoids taxation of capital gains

- 401k employer investment plans – postpones having to   pay taxes on your earned income and capital gains until   money is withdrawn, possibly when your older and in a lower tax bracket

- Tax credit for college education – reduces gross salary income which results in reduced taxation

- Annual retirement withdrawals from IRA's and 401k's when reaching 59.5 years of age that have tax advantage incentives.

The term "qualified investments" is used for the forementioned retirement savings plans because they "qualify" for a delay in paying taxes on the money invested, until the time of withdrawal.

Summary:

The more you know about ways to avoid paying or delaying tax levies, the faster your nest egg will accumulate.

Chapter 3

Real-Estate

Everyone needs to have a place to live. Owning your home not only provides you with a roof over your head and the ability to live with the rules you set for the household, but it also sets up an opportunity to increase your net worth by owning a very large tangible asset. Over years of owning real estate, my homes have increased in market value, similar to how the stock market has always moved in an upward trend over time. So, if you use a loan to purchase your home, like most people do, over time you will increase the amount of equity (net value of home after paying off any liabilities) you own by paying down the mortgage. Location of a property demands careful consideration, but the value of one's home generally increases over time.

For your first home, buying a two-family home can potentially speed up the ability to increase wealth. This is a way to have another party pay the monthly mortgage, or at least help with paying the mortgage, thereby speeding up the ability to build equity/wealth thru increased mortgage payments or freeing up cash for other investments. If you know of a trustworthy individual interested in buying a two-family home with you, such as a sibling, then you can both help one another pay the mortgage and take care of the maintenance of the home.

It's important to know that the capital gains (profit), on the sale of a personal home, is that the first $250,000 is free from federal taxes on the portion of the home that is your living unit. So, when selling a two-family home, the capital gains on the half you occupied would be tax exempt. However, you most hold the house for at least five years, and have lived in it for at least two consecutive years. If you are married, the tax write off is doubled to $500,000 on capital gains.

Another wealth building strategy exists if you are handy at fixing things around the house, or if you are good at learning how to fix things and take on the challenge. Sweat equity, working to fix your home, can be a huge way to increase the value of your home and reduce costs.

Chapter 4

Credit Rating

There are three major credit rating agencies monitoring personal financial transactions. Experian, Equifax, and Transunion are business organizations which significantly affect credit ratings. The credit score they determine for an individual can affect the cost of car insurance, rates of interest on loans, the ability to obtain credit, and many other financial transactions that have an impact on our ability to accumulate wealth.

A typical credit rating scale has a maximum score of 850; this is also commonly referred to as your FICO score. FICO is an acronym for Fair Issac Corporation, the company instrumental in developing the credit rating method for evaluating the financial history of individuals. Having a score of about 750 or more (highest score category), usually translates to getting the best financial deals with insurance companies and banks.

Usually there are six factors or categories that affect your credit rating; payment history, length of time with an established credit history, credit usage, balances, credit checks, and available credit. The first three factors have a high impact on your credit score, while the last three have a lower impact on your credit score. Although each factor has a different amount of influence on your score, all of them should be kept under careful control throughout your financial years.

Suggestion: Open a credit card account as soon as possible. Make sure you use your credit card responsibly, and keep this credit card open for as long as possible. Pay off your balance each month to avoid paying high interest rates on the line of credit. Establishing credit and the length of time holding the credit account has a significant impact on your credit score.

Chapter 5

Credit Cards

Owning credit cards can be an effective way of reducing

traveling costs if they are used responsibly, meaning that the

full monthly balance is paid off before the due date. Many

credit cards backed by banks have a business relationship

with hotels and airlines that offer travel reward points which can be used to save thousands of dollars on hotel and airline tickets. Typically, the best bonus deals occur when you initially sign up for the credit card and spend a predetermined amount of money, in a certain amount of time (i.e. often times $3,000 dollars in three months from the opening of the account). As per the credit card agreement, you will then be awarded a substantial amount of bonus reward points. These bonus award points typically range between 10,000 and 100,000 points, worth between $100.00 to $1,500.00 dollars as cash rewards and travel rewards.

Churning credit cards can be an effective way of saving thousands of dollars over time. This is the process of obtaining several different cards that offer bonus points and continuous reward points every month, based on your monthly spending. Consider cancelling some of these cards after a year or more, in order to maximize the more generous rewards usually offered when initially signing up, remembering to spend the required amount within the specified time to qualify for the signing bonus. Typically, there is a two-year waiting period for the same credit card offer before qualifying for the initial bonus award points again. Some credit card initial sign-up bonus offers are only allowed once in a lifetime. You must take the time to read the fine print for each credit card offer in order to maximize and qualify for the rewards. It can be tricky navigating the rules of each credit card agreement, but following them can save thousands of dollars over the years and increase your wealth over time.

Remember one very important rule, always pay credit cards in full by the due date. Credit card interest rates run as high as 30% or more, and late fees of up to $30.00 or more can be added on. Paying these high rates and fees is like throwing money out of your car window as it's moving, don't do it!

The exception to this rule is a credit card offer with a promotion for free interest on purchases for a certain amount of time. As long as the minimum amount due is paid each billing period, you have an interest free loan. When the free interest time period is up, the card should be paid in full. If it's not paid in full, high interest rates will be assessed.

Chapter 6

Stock, Bonds, Mutual Funds and Exchange Traded Funds

The United States has the largest economy in the world. The

U.S. dollar is traded and used globally in many countries. The

two major U.S. stock markets are the New York Stock

Exchange, and the NASDAQ stock exchange, an acronym for

National Association of Securities Dealers Automatic

Quotation System. These two stock markets are rated the

largest and second largest markets in the world, respectively.

In addition, there is also a smaller stock trading platform

called the Pink Sheets (also known as the over-the-counter

market), which lists many highly speculative securities for

non-mature companies. Since Pink Sheet trading is very

speculative (less regulated than the other major markets), it

is safer and recommended to trade in the previously

mentioned markets.

Mature companies have provided investors opportunities to

expand wealth by allowing individuals to become

shareholders in their companies. These mature companies

consistently produce net revenues that either increase the

value of the stock (capital gain/stock appreciation), or

provide cash disbursements to shareholders (dividends).

A common way that many individuals get involved with the stock market is through mutual funds. These funds are equities managed by financial corporations that bundle several different corporation's equities, such as stocks and bonds, and even government treasuries, etc. to broaden the investors investment in the stock market. Mutual funds can provide an averaging effect by eliminating the spikes (up or down) of one's individual stock or bond. These investment options are typically offered by the companies that people work for via 401k investing plans, or any other type of tax privileged retirement plan. Companies hire investment corporations to manage their retirement plans. An individual can also access mutual funds through their own investment broker.

Bonds are investment vehicles put out by governments and corporations to raise money. They are basically a loan given to the government or corporation by the investor for a specified period of time and specified interest rate. Bonds are rated based on the originating entities' ability to pay them back, which takes into account the entities' financial stability.

U.S. government issued I-bonds pay investors variable interest, and are considered a very safe investment. The interest rate on an I-bond has gone as high as 10% in recent times.

Another investment option that has gained popularity in recent times are ETFs (Exchange-traded funds). They are similar to mutual funds, bundling assets (securities) within a fund which are traded on stock exchanges throughout the day. They can track a particular index (i.e. DOW30), or be invested in almost any combination of stocks, bonds, treasuries, etc.

There are several ways to invest in the stock and bond markets, each having their pros and cons. An investor should consider tax implications on both the investment gains and the potential to reduce taxes on an individuals' current salary. There are tax incentives for investing in qualified retirement accounts, commonly referred to as tax deferred investing. Please refer to Chapter 2 – Taxes, for examples of tax saving/tax deferred retirement accounts.

Chapter 7

Insurance

Insurance premiums can be a substantial but necessary expense to hedge against large losses. There are several main categories of insurance that must be considered throughout our financial journey, these include: medical, dental, optical, housing, and automotive insurances. Two other insurance categories that should be considered include life and disability insurance, and possibly umbrella insurance.

Keeping a good credit rating is one way to minimize the premiums for your insurance needs.

Everyone's consideration of the aforementioned insurance categories are different based on several factors, such as whether or not you own a home, have a job that provides benefits, and if you own a vehicle. Your marriage status and whether or not you have kids or has a large impact on insurance decisions. Thousands can be saved when you find a job that provides employer contributions towards some of these important insurance coverages.

Between employer provided benefits and a good credit score, several of the insurance categories can have substantially reduced premiums.

Other ways to reduce insurance premiums include getting at least three insurance quotes, reviewing your policies once a year to make sure the premiums are not dramatically increasing, raising the deductible on the policy, and generally opting for term versus whole life insurance.

One very important insurance that should be known to all is FDIC (Federal Deposit Insurance Corporation) insurance. This United States government corporation provides free replacement coverage for bank deposits up to $250,000.00 for each account should your bank go bankrupt.

In the event you do your banking at a credit union, NCUA (National Credit Union Association) insurance is exists, which mimics FDIC insurance.

FDIC and NCUA insurance are also discussed in Chapter 9 – Banks and Credit Unions.

Chapter 8

Health, Dress, and Organization

It's imperative that we maintain both our mental and physical health. Having a healthy frame of mind and good physical health, enables the ability to function and operate efficiently in everyday events, including the use of wealth building skills. It's important to be able to keep earning a living through a job, instead of spending large amounts of time and resources on restoring ourselves from bad health.

Preventative measures to keep our bodies functioning at a high level include good eating habits, regular sleep, and repetitive exercise. Reading informative periodicals, newspapers, and books helps keep the mind actively learning and healthy. The power of a healthy mind and body significantly enhances the ability of an individual to increase wealth.

The way we present ourselves to other individuals has a major impact on our everyday lives, especially when we are seeking a new job opportunity, selling ourselves or a company product.   Having a refreshed look and professional appearance is an excellent way to start any relationship, meeting, job interview, presentation, or sales pitch. First encounters and impressions matter in our daily lives. Dress for success! Your personal appearance influences the perception of your credibility.

Good organizational skills create the ability to be efficient
and effective. We all have had days when we are unable to
find tools, objects, or information needed to carry out a task,
adding to the time required to get a job done. This reduces
efficiency and makes us look less competent.

Chapter 9

Banks and Credit Unions

To establish credit and have a safe place to keep money,
banks are an obvious choice. The most utilized accounts at
banks are both checking and savings accounts, as well as CD's
(certificates of deposits). Interest rates offered for the

aforementioned are an important factor in deciding which bank to do business with. However, there are other factors that should be strongly considered when deciding which bank to put your hard-earned money into. These factors include such things as: number and locations of ATM's and branches, bonus promotions for setting up an account, and the fees associated with banking privileges (i.e. non-bank ATM use fees, monthly minimum balance fees, cashier check fees, and other bank related activity fees). Evaluating a bank's fees and services based on your financial situation can maximize your earnings.

There are times when switching banks or having multiple accounts in several banks is important. Capitalizing on banking promotions can be lucrative. Sign up bonuses can reach up to $1200.00 when opening new bank accounts. They usually require maintaining a minimum balance and a direct deposit of a portion of your paycheck into the accounts.

It should also be noted that an individual can save thousands of dollars in mailing fees over a lifetime when banking on-line. Also, the time saved not having to address envelopes and attach stamps is a bonus.

Credit Unions, defined as non-profit financial cooperatives, have similar investment options to banks. They are owned by the members (owners of the credit union accounts) and governed by a board of directors.

Bank accounts (savings, checking, and CD's) are FDIC insured up to certain limits. Credit Union accounts are insured by the NCUA (National Credit Union Association), like the FDIC insurance for banks.

Chapter 10

Buying and Maintaining a Vehicle

The purchase of a vehicle is one of the more expensive purchases for an individual to make in a lifetime, and it will likely happen multiple times during your life. The useful life of a car is about 12 years, plus or minus a couple of years depending on how many miles your vehicle is driven per year. With this in mind, and figuring a human lifespan of 80 years, we may end up buying as many as 6 new vehicles or more over a lifetime. However, if we buy used vehicles instead and keep them from 3 to 5 years, we may end up buying about 15 cars over our lifespan.

Due to deprecation, vehicles are one of the worst assets for accumulating wealth for most people. A brand-new car loses a huge percent of its value in the first three years of use. Depending on which brand new vehicle you buy, it can depreciate in value a minimum of 10% to 40% per year over the first three years, and continue to lose 15% to 20% over the next few years after the initial three years. The rate of depreciation typically declines as the vehicle gets older. Buying something 3-5 years old can save a fortune in the cost of depreciation over time while owning the vehicle, and still obtain several years of its useful life.

Proper maintenance of your automobile is critical for your transportation needs and avoids prematurely needing to buy another vehicle. An inexpensive way to help keep your car in good running order is to routinely change your oil. Finding a good mechanic that works out of his home or garage can save a fortune in automotive repair bills. I have saved thousands on repair bills over the years by hiring people that like to fix cars and make a few bucks doing it.

Chapter 11

Helpful Suggestions

- It's not how much you make, it's how much you spend.

- Getting started as early as possible on saving for retirement lengthens the ability to compound interest and to enhance savings.

- Dollar cost average your investing, which means investing weekly or biweekly as your get your paycheck. Use automatic deductions from your paycheck to invest in an employer's 401K retirement plan, or any type of retirement plan your employer offers. At a minimum, invest at least enough to meet the amount your employer matches. Avoid investing a 100% of your nest egg into your company's stock.

- Diversify investing within your company's retirement plan

- Paying one extra mortgage payment per year on a typical 30-year fixed mortgage can reduce the length of the loan term to 16 years.

- Get more than one quote for automotive insurance, housing repairs, and other insurance needs.

- View the internet to learn how to fix things.

- Use the right credit card to cover auto rental insurance (instead of paying extra at the rental agency), to avoid foreign transaction fees, to obtain free travel insurance, and for free purchase protection.

- Pay your credit card balances in full each month, paying high-rate credit card interest is one of the worst financial mistakes.

- Buy a used car instead of a new one (reduces depreciation loss), and use cash to purchase (eliminates financing interest), unless the company you work for pays for your vehicle.

- Don't put all your eggs in one basket, instead diversify.

- Live within your means. Take seriously the difference between needs and wants.

- Have reasonable budgets for entertainment, vacations, and recreational expenses.

- Coupons are like paper money, use them when you can.

- Dress for success.

- Read a book.

- Do a crossword puzzle, or a word game.

- Exercise regularly.

- Avoid get rich quick schemes and tame or give up bad habits like drinking, smoking, and gambling.

Chapter 12

Social Security

Social Security benefits provide monthly payments to workers and their families based on a worker's lifetime earnings and work history. The benefits are calculated using an "average indexed monthly earnings" (AIME) that considers up to 35 years of a worker's highest earnings, adjusted for wage levels. You can apply for benefits starting at age 62, but the amount increases the longer you wait to file, up to age 70. 🔗

How Benefits are Calculated 🔗

1. **AIME Calculation:** The Social Security Administration (SSA) first "indexes" your past earnings to reflect

changes in general wage levels during your employment.

2. **35-Year Average:** They then select your 35 years with the highest indexed earnings, sum them, and divide by the total number of months in those years to get your AIME.

3. **Primary Insurance Amount (PIA):** A formula is applied to your AIME to determine your PIA, which is the basis for your monthly benefit.

Types of Benefits

- **Retirement Benefits**: You can apply for these anytime between age 62 and 70. ⬦
-
Family Benefits: These provide payments to eligible family members, such as spouses or children, of a retired or disabled worker. ⬦

- **Survivor Benefits**: Provide monthly payments to eligible family members of a deceased worker. ⬦

- **Disability Benefits (SSDI)**: Provide payments to workers who have a disability. ⬦
-
Supplemental Security Income (SSI): A separate program that provides benefits based on income and resources, not on work history. ⬦

Factors Affecting Your Benefits

- **Age of Claiming**: Waiting longer to claim your benefits (up to age 70) results in a higher monthly payment. 🔗

- **Earnings History**: Higher lifetime earnings lead to higher benefits. 🔗

- **Taxes and Medicare**: Medicare Part B premiums are often deducted from your monthly check, and you may owe income taxes on your benefits. 🔗

Where to Get More Information

- **my Social Security Account**: You can create an account to see a personalized estimate of your benefits, based on your actual earnings history. 🔗

- **Social Security Administration (SSA) Website**: The SSA's official website, ssa.gov, offers detailed information on benefit calculations, claiming options, and online tools to manage your account.

Retirement Ready

ssa.gov

Fact Sheet For Workers Ages 61-69

Retirement is different for everyone

Because retirement is not one-size-fits-all, we want to provide you with the information you need to plan for retirement and to make informed decisions.

You have choices to make

Some of these decisions may involve your Social Security retirement benefits. You can continue to work, apply for benefits, do both, or do neither. Each choice comes with important considerations for you and your family. Learn about them at *ssa.gov/benefits/retirement/matrix.html*.

Your "full" retirement age

Depending on when you were born, your full retirement age could be from 66 to 67. Find your exact full retirement age at

Example Only

Age Retirement Benefits Start	Monthly Benefit Amount
62	$750
63	$800
64	$866
65	$933
66	$1,000
67	$1,080
68	$1,160
69	$1,240
70	$1,320

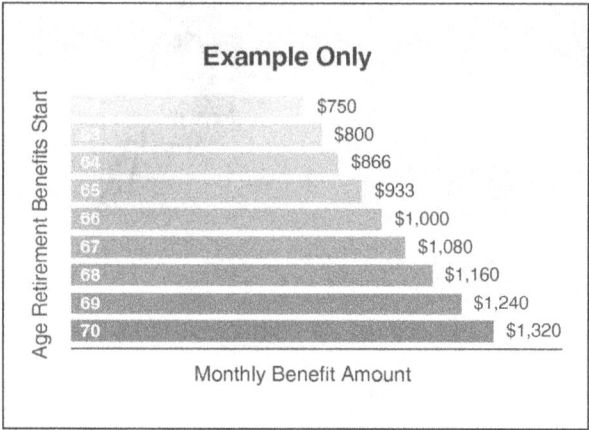

ssa.gov/planners/retire/retirechart.html.

When you start affects how much you get

Everyone's decision about when to start receiving benefits is different. Say that your monthly benefit at a full retirement age of 66 is $1,000. Starting retirement benefits early at 62 or late at 70 can mean the difference between $750 and $1,320 a month. The graph on this page gives you an example. Your *Social Security Statement* provides your personalized retirement benefit estimates.

Earnings are essential

Your earnings are used to determine your eligibility for Social Security benefits and your benefit amount. Use your *Social Security Statement* to check your earnings each year. If you see an error on your earnings record, report it to us. Learn how at *ssa.gov/pubs/EN-05-10081.pdf*.

Benefits last as long as you live

Your benefits last as long as you live. Taking benefits before your full retirement age (as early as age 62) lowers the amount you get each month. Delaying benefits past full retirement age (up to age 70) increases the monthly amount for the rest of your life. Our Life Expectancy Calculator can provide a rough estimate of how long you might live based on your age and sex: *ssa.gov/planners/lifeexpectancy.html*.

Benefits are protected from inflation

Your benefit will be adjusted to keep up with inflation. Learn about these cost-of-living adjustments (COLAs) at *ssa.gov/cola*.

Some benefits are taxed

You may have to pay federal income taxes on a portion of your Social Security benefits if you have other substantial income in addition to your benefits (such as wages, self-employment, interest, dividends, and other taxable income that must be reported on your tax return). You may choose to have federal income taxes withheld from your Social Security benefit. Learn more at *ssa.gov/planners/taxes.html*.

Working while getting benefits

If you get retirement benefits but want to continue to work, you can. However, depending on how much you earn before full retirement age, we might temporarily withhold all or some of your benefit amount. When you reach full retirement age, we will recalculate your benefit amount to give you credit for the months we reduced or withheld benefits due to your excess earnings. Any earnings after you reach your full retirement age won't reduce your benefits. Learn more at *ssa.gov/pubs/EN-05-10069.pdf*.

Work may boost your benefits

Your earnings can increase your monthly benefit amount — even after you start receiving benefits. Each year, we check your earnings record if you continue to work. If your latest year of earnings turns out to be one of your highest 35 years, we will automatically recalculate your benefit amount and pay you any increase due. You can get additional estimates based on what you think your future earnings will be with the *my* Social Security Retirement Calculator at *myaccount.ssa.gov*.

Avoid a Medicare penalty

Even if you delay retirement benefits, be sure to sign up for Medicare three months before you turn 65 to avoid the lifelong penalty. Special rules apply if you are covered by a health plan at work. Find out about Medicare, including the different parts of Medicare, the coverage options, how to apply, and how to avoid a lifelong penalty at *ssa.gov/pubs/EN-05-10043.pdf*.

Unable to work due to a mental or physical disability

You may be able to receive Social Security disability benefits if you are unable to work at a certain earnings level due to a mental or physical disability, have not reached full retirement age, and if you meet certain eligibility requirements. Learn more about disability benefits at *ssa.gov/disability*. The Supplemental Security Income (SSI) program pays benefits to adults and children with disabilities who have limited income and resources. Learn more about SSI at *ssa.gov/benefits/ssi/* .

Benefits for family members

Your family, including your spouse, former spouses, and dependent children, may qualify for benefits on your record. Find out more about benefits for your family at *ssa.gov/benefits/retirement/planner/applying7.html*.

Your family may also be eligible for survivors benefits. If you are the higher earning spouse, your decision on when to claim benefits can affect the benefits of your surviving spouse. Find out more about survivors benefits at *ssa.gov/planners/survivors*.

Benefits as a spouse

If you are married, divorced, or widowed, you may be eligible for higher benefits on your spouse's record. When you apply for either retirement or spousal benefits, you may be required to apply for both benefits at the same time. Learn more at *ssa.gov/pubs/EN-05-10035.pdf*.

Understanding your retirement benefits

Social Security is not meant to be your only source of income in retirement. On average, Social Security will replace about 40% of your annual pre-retirement earnings, although this can vary based on each person's circumstances. Learn more at *ssa.gov/planners/retire*.

We are here for you

Social Security covers about 96% of American workers. To learn more about Social Security, visit *ssa.gov*.

Chapter 13

Medicare

Understanding Medicare

Medicare is a federal health insurance program for people age 65 or older, certain people under 65 with disabilities, and people of any age with End-Stage Renal Disease (ESRD) (permanent kidney failure requiring dialysis or a kidney transplant).

The Centers for Medicare & Medicaid Services (CMS) manages the Medicare program. There are different parts to the Medicare program. Social Security takes applications for and enrolls people in Parts A and B. Private insurance companies take applications for and provide coverage under Part C (Medicare Advantage), Part D (Prescription Drug

Coverage), and the Medicare Supplemental Insurance program (Medigap). This document explains some of the options you may have when choosing your Medicare coverage. Note that if you choose not to enroll in Medicare Parts B or D when first eligible and then decide to enroll later, **you may have to pay higher monthly premiums, also known as a late enrollment penalty, for as long as you have coverage.** Also, you may have to wait for a "Special Enrollment Period" to enroll in Part B, which may delay this coverage. You may have to wait for an Open Enrollment Period to enroll in Part D.

Parts of Medicare

Medicare helps with the cost of health care, *but it may not cover all medical expenses and does not cover the cost of long-term care when it's the only care you need*. This section explains the different parts of Medicare and the services they cover.

Original Medicare (Parts A and B)
Medicare Advantage (Part C)

Original Medicare Includes:

☑ Part A

☑ Part B

You can add:

☐ Part D

☐ Supplemental Coverage

Medicare Advantage includes:

☑ Part A

☑ Part B

Most plans also include:

☑ Part D

☑ Extra Benefits

Part A (Hospital Insurance) helps pay for inpatient care in a hospital or for a limited time at a skilled nursing facility (following a hospital stay). Part A also pays for some home health care and hospice care.

Part B (Medical Insurance) helps pay for services from doctors and other health care providers, outpatient care, home health care, durable medical equipment, and some preventive services. After you meet your deductible for the year, you typically pay 20% of the Medicare-approved amount for most of these services.

Part D (Prescription Drug Coverage) helps cover the cost of prescription drugs and many shots and vaccines.

Medicare Supplemental Insurance Program (Medigap) is extra insurance you can buy from a private company that helps pay your share of costs in Original Medicare.

Medicare Advantage (Medicare Part C) is a "bundled" plan, offered by Medicare-approved private companies, that includes all benefits and services covered under Parts A and B, usually Part D, and may include additional benefits such as vision, hearing, and dental.

Your Medicare Enrollment Options

If you're getting benefits from Social Security or the Railroad Retirement Board (RRB) at least 4 months before you turn 65, you'll automatically get Part A and Part B when you turn 65. If you live in Puerto Rico, you automatically get Part A, and if you want Part B, you'll need to sign up for it. If you're not getting benefits from Social Security or the RRB at least 4 months before you turn 65, you'll need to sign up with Social Security to get Part A and Part B. If you're getting benefits, your Part B premium will get deducted automatically from your benefit payment, and if not, you'll get a bill from Medicare to pay your premiums. You may delay signing up for Part B if you qualify for a Special Enrollment Period: *ssa.gov/pubs/EN-05-10012.pdf*. If you're under 65 and have a disability, you'll automatically get Part A and Part B after you get disability benefits from Social Security, or certain disability benefits from the RRB, for 24 months.

You can choose one of two ways to get Medicare coverage:

Original Medicare

- Includes Medicare Part A (Hospital Insurance) and Part B (Medical Insurance).

- If you have a work history, you most likely will not pay a premium for Medicare Part A because of Medicare taxes you paid while working.

- You will pay monthly premiums for Medicare Parts B and D, and Medigap, unless you qualify for a low-income subsidy.

- If you want drug coverage, you can join a separate Medicare drug plan (Part D).
- To help pay your out-of-pocket costs in Original Medicare (like your 20% coinsurance), you can also shop for and buy supplemental coverage, like Medigap or insurance from a private company.
- You can use any doctor or hospital that takes Medicare, anywhere in the U.S.
- **The cost of the Part B late enrollment penalty increases the longer you go without Part B coverage or employer group health insurance.** Your Part B monthly premium will go up 10% for each 12-month period you were eligible but did not enroll. If you have group health insurance and work for an employer with 20 or more employees, you can delay Medicare Part B without penalty.

The cost of the Part D late enrollment penalty depends on how long you went without Part D or creditable prescription drug coverage. Your Part D late enrollment penalty is 1% of the national base beneficiary premium multiplied by the number of months you were eligible but didn't join a Medicare drug plan. Usually, you don't pay a penalty if you had other creditable prescription drug coverage. To be creditable, the coverage must pay, on average, at least as much as Medicare's standard prescription coverage.

- Learn more about **Original Medicare** at *ssa.gov/benefits/medicare*.

Medicare Advantage (also known as Part C)

- Medicare Advantage is an "all in one" alternative to Original Medicare. These "bundled" plans include Part A, Part B, and usually Part D.

- You must first be enrolled in Original Medicare before you can choose to switch to a Medicare Advantage plan.
- Plans may have lower out-of-pocket costs than Original Medicare.
- In most cases, you'll need to use doctors who are in the plan's network.
- Most plans offer extra benefits that Original Medicare doesn't cover—like vision, hearing, dental, and more.
- Coverage is provided by private insurance companies approved by Medicare.
- In addition to the monthly premium for Part B, Medicare Advantage plans may charge an additional premium for the extra benefits they offer.
- Learn more about **Medicare Advantage** at *Medicare.gov/Pubs/pdf/12026-UnderstandingMedicare-Advantage-Plans.pdf*.

www.ingramcontent.com/pod-product-compliance
Lightning Source LLC
Chambersburg PA
CBHW050514210326
41521CB00011B/2451